LEGACIES

from

ANCIENT CHINA

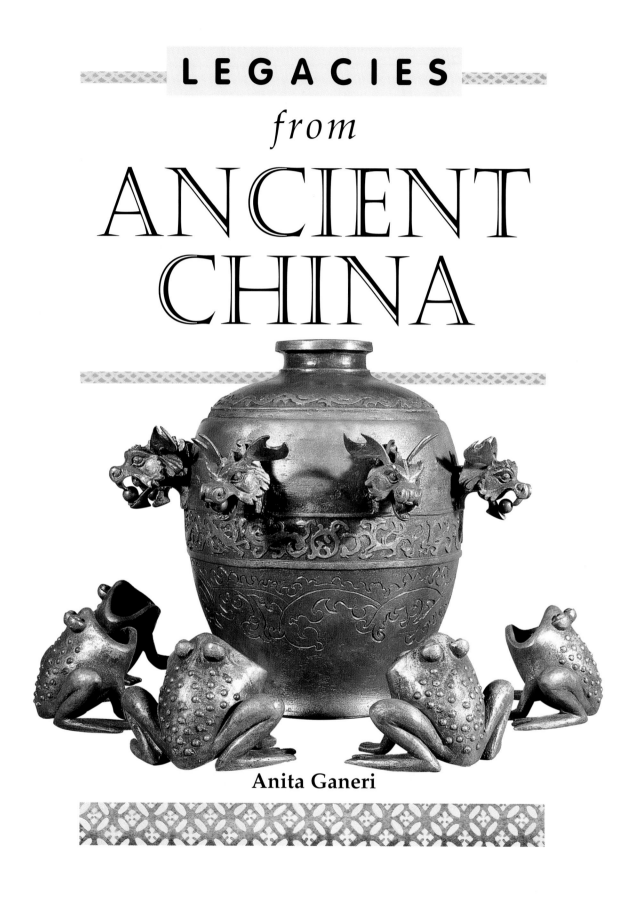

Anita Ganeri

Belitha Press

First published in the UK in 1999 by

 Belitha Press Limited, London House,
Great Eastern Wharf, Parkgate Road,
London SW11 4NQ

ISBN 1 84138 026 1

British Library Cataloguing in Publication Data for
this book is available from the British Library.

Printed in China

Editor: Veronica Ross
Designer: Rosamund Saunders
Picture Researcher: Diana Morris
Consultant: Sallie Purkis
Illustrator: Jackie Harland

PHOTO CREDITS
AAA Collection: 14bl, 22ct & 26bl © R. Sheridan.
AKG London: 5bl, 13tl, 15b Erich Lessing/Gutenberg
Museum, Mainz.
AP/Xinhua: 23tr.
Axiom: 29bl Gordon D.R. Clements.
Bridgeman Art Library: 3t, 7bl British Museum, 26cl Stapleton
Collection UK, 28bl Oriental Bronzes Ltd. London.
British Library, London: 17tl, 18br.
Corbis: 11c Keren Su, 17bl © Craig Aurness/Westlight.
ET Archive: front cover b, 6c British Library, 8b, 8r British Library,
10bl Victoria & Albert Museum, 12c British Museum, 12br, 15c
British Library, 23br & 29cr Bibliotheque Nationale Paris.
Werner Forman Archive: back cover, 2, 7c, 9cr British Museum,
11bl. Art Gallery of NSW Sydney, 28br Private Collection.
Robert Harding PL: 3b, 4cr, 5cr, 6l, 13c G. Corrigan, 19tl Rudy
Tesa/Int'l Stock, 21br, 24br G. Corrigan, 27b.
Michael Holford/Science Museum, London: 1, 7tl, 5b, 26c.
Hutchison PL: 22cr Juliet Highet, 28cr Nancy Durrell McKenna.
SPL: 17cr John Howard, 26cr David Parker.
Science & Society PL: 22bl Science Museum, London.
Tony Stone: 30cr Bob Thomas.
Trip: front cover t, 4bl H & J Blackwell, 9bl Coyote Fotografx,
10cr J. Stanley, 14cr G Howe, 19bl J. Moscrop, 20br D. Morgan,
30l D Houghton.

THE DATES IN THIS BOOK
BC (Before Christ) is used with dates of events that
happened before the birth of Christ. AD (Anno Domini,
from the latin for 'in the year of our Lord') is used with
dates of events that happened after the birth of Christ.
The letter c used in the text stands for the Latin word
circa, and means about.

Some of the more unfamiliar words used in this book
are explained in the glossary on page 30.

CONTENTS

INTRODUCTION

A legacy is something handed down from one person or generation to another. It may be an object, a lifestyle or a way of thinking. The Ancient Chinese lived centuries ago, yet the legacy of their amazing culture lives on today. They were brilliant scientists and inventors, with a technology far ahead of the rest of the world. Among many other things, they invented the compass, gunpowder, paper, printing, silk, porcelain and tea drinking – legacies which changed the world.

IMPACT

The skill of the craftworkers of Ancient China and the luxurious lifestyles of its early rulers are still admired today. One of China's most famous tourist attractions is the Terracotta Army. This is made up of thousands of life-sized, clay warriors buried over 2000 years ago to guard the tomb of China's first emperor, Qin Shi Huangdi. It was rediscovered in 1974.

Soldiers of the Terracotta Army.

◄ *Life in the Chinese countryside has not changed much in thousands of years. This farmer is ploughing his fields with an ox-drawn plough just as his ancestors did.*

Early China

The earliest Chinese civilizations grew up along the banks of three rivers – the Huang He (Yellow River), Chang Jiang (Yangtze River) and Xi Jiang (West River). Farming communities date back to about 5000 BC. Rice was grown along the Chang Jiang from about 4000 BC. It is still the staple crop, and food, of China.

The Middle Kingdom

High mountains, vast plains and desert lie to the north and west of China; to the south and east is the sea. In ancient times, this meant that China was almost completely cut off from the rest of the world. For centuries its culture developed quite independently, away from outside influences. The Chinese called their country Zhong-Guo, the Middle Kingdom. They believed that it lay in the middle of the universe, at the very centre of civilization.

▲ This map shows Ancient China and its position in South-East Asia.

In 1968, Chinese soldiers made an extraordinary discovery – the tombs of Prince Liu Sheng and Princess Dou Wan who died in the early second century BC. Their tombs were full of treasures. Most spectacular of all were the two priceless jade suits in which the royal couple were buried. Each suit was made of thousands of tiny pieces of jade, sewn together with gold thread.

The jade funeral suit of Princess Dou Wan.

◄ *Chinese archaeologists restoring the terracotta soldiers guarding Qin Shi Huangdi's tomb. The army was discovered by workmen digging a well.*

How do we know?

Our knowledge of life in Ancient China comes from many different sources. There are written records on bone, silk and paper, and paintings showing scenes from everyday life. Some wealthy Chinese people were buried in tombs with clothes, weapons, jewellery, pottery models, and even food and drink, for use in the next life. From these objects, archaeologists have built up a fascinating picture of what Ancient Chinese life was like.

KEY DATES IN

| 5000 BC | 2000 BC | 1000 BC | 200 BC |

c 5000 BC The first farming settlements are established along the Huang He.

c 2205-1766 BC The traditional dates for the Xia Dynasty, said to be the very first Chinese dynasty. No one knows if the Xia really existed or not.

c 551-479 BC Life of the philosopher, Confucius.

1027-221 BC The Zhou Dynasty rules. This is a time of growth in overseas trade and in the economy.
Sixth century BC. Iron working is introduced. Life of the philosopher, Laozi.

475-221 BC The Warring States Period. Seven major states struggle for power.

210 BC Death of Qin Shi Huangdi.

202 BC Liu Bang becomes the first emperor of the Han Dynasty. This is a time of great artistic and scientific activity, during which paper is invented. This first period of Han rule is called the Former Han.

221 BC Qin Shi Huangdi, the first ruler of the Qin Dynasty, proclaims himself the first emperor of China. He unites China for the first time and introduces standard laws and systems of money, weights and measures. He also standardizes Chinese script.

1766-1027 BC The Shang Dynasty rules. The first known examples of Chinese writing are found on Shang oracle bones. The Bronze Age begins in China.

214-204 BC The Great Wall of China is extended and joined to protect the northern border.

206 BC Qin Shi Huangdi's son is defeated by Liu Bang.

ANCIENT CHINA

AD 25 AD 500 AD 900 AD 1300

AD 9-25 Wang Mang seizes control of China and establishes a short-lived dynasty.

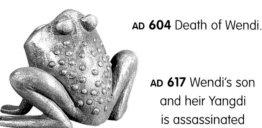

AD 604 Death of Wendi.

AD 907 The fall of the Tang Dynasty.

AD 25 Wang Mang is overthrown and the Han take control again. This second period of Han rule is called the Later Han.

AD 617 Wendi's son and heir Yangdi is assassinated and the Sui overthrown.

AD 907-960 China splits into five kingdoms. Five emperors try to reunite the country and start a new dynasty, but none succeed.

AD 618 The Tang Dynasty begins. Chinese art and poetry flourish, and many advances are made in science and technology.

AD 960 Emperor Zhao Kuang Yin founds the Song Dynasty.

AD 220 The end of Han rule. The empire splits into three kingdoms – Wu, Shu and Wei.

AD 979 Zhao Kuang Yin's brother reunites China.

AD 1126 Northern China is overrun by invaders. The Song lose control of the north and the emperor and his family are taken prisoner. One son escapes and becomes ruler of a new empire in the south, called the Southern Song Dynasty.

AD 380s China is divided into the Northern and Southern kingdoms.

AD 581 Wendi, the ruler of the Northern kingdom, founds the Sui Dynasty and sets out to reunite China for the first time since the fall of the Han.

AD 1279 The last of the Song emperors is defeated by the Mongols, a war-like, nomadic people from Mongolia. Their leader, Kublai Khan, becomes emperor of China. He rules until his death in 1294.

AD 589 China is reunified.

THE STORY OF CHINA

From about 2205 BC, China was ruled by a series of dynasties, or ruling families. The first for which we have real evidence is the Shang Dynasty which began in about 1766 BC. It was conquered at the end of the eleventh century BC by the Zhou. Their rule lasted until 221 BC. The Zhou's lands were divided into many small states which were constantly at war. In the middle of the third century BC, the state of Qin took control. In 221 BC, the Qin ruler, Qin Shi Huangdi, became the first emperor of China.

Qin Shi Huangdi, the first emperor of China.

◄ *A bronze container for wine. It was made during the Shang dynasty.*

8

IMPACT

Emperor Qin Shi Huangdi's legacy lives on in our name for China. This comes from the first part of his name, which is sometimes spelled Ch'in. We also use the word china to mean the very fine porcelain pottery produced by the Ancient Chinese (see page 27).

The rise of the Qin

Under Qin Shi Huangdi's rule, China was united for the first time. He standardized the country's laws, money, script, and weights and measures. Until then each state had its own system which was very confusing. The system of government which Qin Shi Huangdi set in place stayed almost unchanged for the next 2000 years.

The Han Dynasty

From 202 BC to AD 220, China was ruled by the Han Dynasty. Chinese culture flourished. Among the greatest inventions of this time were the magnetic compass, the ship's rudder and paper. But the population grew so much that many peasant farmers were left without land and began to rebel. This, and attacks by Mongol nomads in the north, weakened the government and the empire collapsed.

◄ We know a lot about China in Han times from objects found buried in Han tombs. This stone model shows a palace gate.

Later dynasties

After the Han Dynasty, China split into three kingdoms. In AD 581, Emperor Wendi seized the throne of the northern kingdom, founded the Sui Dynasty and began to reunite the country. In 618, the Sui were followed by the Tang Dynasty, a time of excellence in science, technology and the arts. In 960, the first Song emperor came to the throne, and China became prosperous. But in 1279, the Song were conquered by Mongol invaders from the north.

◄ A motorcycle and satellite dish give this traditional Mongolian yurt, or tent, a thoroughly modern look!

THE STORY OF SILK

Silk is one of the world's most precious materials, prized for its shine and softness. It was first discovered in China as long ago as 2700 BC, but it was kept a closely-guarded secret for about 3000 years. The punishment for revealing the secret of silk-making was death.

IMPACT

By the first century BC, Chinese silk was exported as far as the Roman Empire. Here it was so valuable, it was worth its weight in gold. By Han times, it had also reached Japan, India, Arabia and Africa. Today, silk is still highly prized. It is often worn on special occasions, such as weddings. The best-quality silks still come from China and India.

Beautiful Chinese silks today.

◄ *This painting shows silk being collected and spun in Ancient China.*

Making silk

Silk is produced by silkworms, the caterpillars of silkworm moths. The silkworms feed on mulberry leaves, then spin silk cocoons around their bodies. Inside the cocoons they change into adults. Each cocoon is made of a single silk thread, up to 900 metres long. In China, the cocoons were dropped into boiling water to make the silk unwind. Then the thread was cleaned and woven into cloth. It takes thousands of cocoons to make one metre of cloth.

The Silk Road

Silk became Ancient China's most valuable export. It was carried to the West by land, along a route called the Silk Road. This ran for about 4000 kilometres from northern China to Antioch, in modern Turkey. In exchange for silk, Chinese traders brought back gold, spices, jewels and jade. It was dangerous work. The road wound through high mountains and dusty deserts. And there was the constant risk of attack from bandits or wild animals.

◀ *Two princesses from the Tang Dynasty wearing long, silk robes which were the height of fashion at that time.*

Legend says that silk-making was discovered by Empress Xi Ling Shi, the wife of a mythical king, Huangdi. The king's gardeners noticed that caterpillars were eating the leaves of the mulberry trees. The empress found a cocoon nearby. She took it inside to study and accidentally dropped it into a bowl of hot water. To her surprise, a fine silk thread began to unwind.

▲ *Silk and other valuable goods were carried along the Silk Road by teams, or caravans, of camels.*

Silk and status

Only rich people could afford silk clothes. They wore long, silk robes tied at the waist with a sash. The colour and pattern of silk showed a person's place in society. Only the emperor and royal family were allowed to wear yellow silk, decorated with dragons. Poor people's clothes were made from coarser plant fibres, such as hemp and nettles.

THE INVENTION OF PAPER

Imagine a world without books, comics or newspapers. Writing, in all shapes and forms, plays an essential part in our lives, as does the paper it is written on. Paper was first made in China in about AD 105 by a government official called Cai Lun. Before that, people wrote on clay, bone, stone, wood, leaves and even silk. But paper became the most important writing material of all.

IMPACT

 The invention of paper led to the first paper money. By the eleventh century, block-printed banknotes were in regular use in China. They replaced the iron coins of the time which were very heavy to carry. Paper money was called 'flying money' because it tended to fly away in the wind.

◀ *The first examples of Chinese writing were found on oracle bones, like this one from the Shang Dynasty. These were animal bones that were used to tell fortunes.*

An early Chinese paper banknote.

▲ *This print shows paper being made in Ancient China. Here the grid is being coated with paper pulp.*

From rags to paper

The first paper was made from rags and chips of bamboo bark. These were mixed with water and beaten into a pulp. A bamboo grid was dipped into the mixture until it was covered in a thin coating of pulp. The excess water was shaken off, and the paper was peeled off the grid. Then the sheet of paper was hung up to dry.

▼ *Paper is still made by hand in China today using traditional, ancient techniques.*

Top secret

Until the seventh century AD, the Chinese kept their discovery top secret. Then it spread to Japan, and to Europe by way of Arabia, where people learnt how to make paper from Chinese prisoners-of-war. The basic Chinese technique of paper-making was used in Europe until the nineteenth century. Paper proved much cheaper and easier to make than parchment made from animal skin.

Chinese characters

In Chinese writing, every symbol, or character, stands for a word or idea. To read and write Chinese well you need to know about 2000 characters, though there are about 50,000 in total. Writing began in China about 4000 years ago. The script was standardized by Emperor Qin Shi Huangdi in 212 BC. It later spread to Korea, Japan and other parts of Asia, where it was adapted to the local languages. Modern Chinese is very similar to the ancient script.

THE PRINTED WORD

Printing was a Chinese invention, known and used in China many years before it reached Western countries. As early as 3000 years ago, the Chinese were using carved stone seals to stamp the signatures of officials on to important documents. By about AD 600, this had developed into a type of printing called block printing.

IMPACT

Before printing was invented, books had to be written out by hand. This was very time consuming and expensive. Today, giant rotary presses are used to print books, newspapers and magazines. These presses are controlled electronically. A modern press can print 75,000 copies of a newspaper in an hour.

A modern newspaper printing press.

◄ *Part of an Ancient Chinese scroll which was block printed.*

Block printing

Block printed books were made using flat wooden blocks, which had pages of text carved on to them so that the characters stood out in reverse and in relief. The blocks were covered in ink, and sheets of paper were pressed on top so that the text was printed the right way round. Illustrations could also be block printed. Printing from wooden blocks was a slow process as a new block was needed for every page in a book.

First printed book

The earliest known printed book is a Chinese scroll called the *Diamond Sutra*. It was block printed in AD 868. It is a Buddhist text containing accounts of the Buddha's life and teaching, illustrated with scenes from the Buddha's life. It is now kept in the British Museum in London.

▲ *A page from the* Diamond Sutra, *a sacred Buddhist text and the world's earliest printed book.*

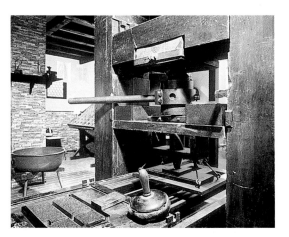

▲ *The printing press invented by Johannes Gutenberg in the fifteenth century.*

Movable type

The next big breakthrough in printing was the invention of movable type. Letters, or characters, were carved on to individual blocks which could then be grouped into lines and pages, and used again and again. Movable type was invented in China in about AD 1040 by a printer called Bi Sheng. In Europe in about 1450, Johannes Gutenberg invented a printing press which used movable metal type.

FINDING THE WAY

The Ancient Chinese were highly skilled scientists, mathematicians and astronomers. From Han times onwards, scientists in the imperial observatories and workshops made some extraordinary discoveries which changed the world forever.

Chinese compass

In about 200 BC, the Chinese discovered that when a lodestone (magnetic rock) floats in water, or hangs freely on a thread, it swings to point in a north-south direction. At first lodestones were used to ensure that houses and temples faced the right way, in harmony with nature. They were later used in simple compasses. The first compasses with dials and pointers were made when it was realized that rubbing a needle on a lodestone gave it magnetic properties.

▶ *Ancient Chinese surveyors using a magnetic compass to choose a suitable site for a building.*

▲ *This beautiful Chinese map shows the walled city of Jiujiang in the province of Jiangxi.*

Master map-makers

Some of the earliest maps come from Ancient China. One was even used in a murder attempt! In 227 BC, Emperor Qin was attacked by a man with a poisoned dagger hidden in a rolled-up map. These early maps were drawn on bamboo or silk. The world's first printed map was made in China in about AD 1155.

A navigator taking a reading from a modern compass.

Steering clear

The ship's rudder was invented in Ancient China in about the second century AD. Archaeologists have found evidence from pottery model ships discovered in Han tombs. Rudders made steering ships much easier and more reliable and allowed the Chinese navy to become the biggest in the world. Before this, sailors used steering oars. These limited the size of ships they could sail and were impossible to control in stormy seas.

◄ *Rudders are still used on the vast majority of modern ships.*

FIGHTING TALK

Most wealthy nobles in Ancient China had their own private armies. Some contained up to one million men. In Shang and Zhou times, warriors fought mostly in chariots drawn by horses. Later armies also included foot soldiers, archers and cavalry. There were many advances in military technology. These included the use of stirrups in the fourth century AD, which gave riders a surer seat and made fighting on horseback easier.

Iron and armour

In Shang times, warriors wore cumbersome suits of armour made of bamboo and wood, padded with cloth. Iron working was discovered in the sixth century BC. This meant that weapons and armour could be made of iron, which was tougher and stronger. Iron armour was essential once crossbows were invented in about 500 BC. In the twelfth century, some armies used thick, pleated paper armour instead. This was good against ordinary arrows, but useless against crossbow bolts. Other weapons included knives, bows and arrows, axes, spears and halberds (blades mounted on long, wooden shafts).

▼ These Ancient Chinese soldiers are shooting arrows from gunpowder-powered rockets.

Ancient explosions

One of the most important Chinese military inventions was gunpowder. It was discovered by accident in the ninth century by a scientist trying to make a potion of everlasting life. The mixture exploded and set fire to his

beard. Gunpowder was made from saltpeter, sulphur and carbon. At first it was used to make fireworks to frighten off the enemy. Explosives are still widely used in modern warfare.

▲ *A bundle of dynamite, a modern type of explosive.*

▼ *In China today rockets are fired into the sky to celebrate festivals and other special occasions.*

Gunpowder power

Gunpowder allowed the Ancient Chinese to have the most advanced weapons of the time. These included grenades and bombs filled with gunpowder and launched from catapults. There were also rockets which shot arrows. The first proper guns were made in AD 1259. These fired pellets from a bamboo tube with a loud bang.

The Great Wall of China.

CHINESE MEDICINE

Today, many people are turning to complementary, or alternative medicine, alongside conventional medicine. There are many different treatments, some of which have developed over thousands of years. They include traditional Chinese medicine, which uses medicines made from natural ingredients, and acupuncture, another ancient Chinese cure.

FAMOUS PEOPLE

By Song times, medicine had become a very respectable profession. In AD 1111, the 12 most brilliant doctors from the Imperial Medical College compiled a huge medical encyclopedia. It set out how illnesses should be recognized, diagnosed and treated. It was one of the first printed medical textbooks.

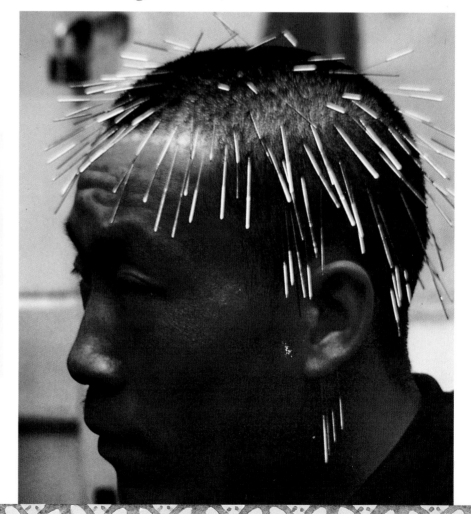

► *A patient being treated using the traditional Chinese technique of acupuncture. It looks painful but it doesn't hurt!*

A healthy balance

The Ancient Chinese believed that everything in the world was controlled by two great opposing forces, called yin and yang. These had to be kept in perfect balance for the world to run smoothly. Illnesses were thought to be caused by yin and yang becoming unbalanced in the body. This balance could be restored by a mixture of herbal medicines, a healthy diet and acupuncture.

▶ This symbol shows yin and yang, the two great forces of the universe which must be kept in harmony.

Pins and needles

Acupuncture has been used in China for about 2000 years. It is based on a belief that your life force runs through your body along 12 lines, called meridians. Each is linked to a different body part. By pushing very fine needles into points on these meridians, you can ease pain and cure illnesses. Today, acupuncture is used all over the world for pain relief and to treat a range of problems from backache to helping people stop smoking. It is also sometimes used in surgery in addition to traditional anaesthetics. Doctors think that it works by encouraging the brain to release natural pain-killing chemicals, called endorphins.

◀ This model shows the 365 acupuncture points of the body. Models like this were used by Chinese doctors to train their students.

A modern Chinese medicine shop.

Wind and water

The Ancient Chinese thought that living in harmony with the world around them was vital to their well being. When planning their towns, they used a set of ideas called Feng Shui, which means wind and water. Every house and street was carefully positioned to keep evil spirits at bay. Today, Feng Shui has become very fashionable with people all over the world.

FLOOD CONTROL

C hinese civilization grew up along three rivers, the Chang Jiang, Huang He and Xi Jiang. Yearly floods made the land more fertile, but bad floods could be disastrous, drowning people and ruining crops. It was essential to control the water, and the imperial engineers worked hard building dams and irrigation canals.

▲ *In modern China flood control is still a serious problem.*

▼ *Emperor Yangdi on his boat on the Grand Canal.*

Canal building

The Ancient Chinese were skilled engineers, building some of the world's first canals. The Chengkuo Canal was opened in 246 BC. It linked two rivers, the Jing and the Luo, and irrigated a vast stretch of land turning it into fertile farmland. Canals were also used to transport goods and people. They were easier to use than roads, and became China's main highways and trading routes.

The Grand Canal

The Grand Canal was begun in Zhou times as a series of small canals linking the Chang Jiang and the Huang He. It was rebuilt under the Sui emperor Yangdi who ruled from AD 604-618. The new canal was wider and deeper. It ran for more than 1100 kilometres, making it possible to travel from north to south avoiding the dangerous sea route. The emperor celebrated the opening of the canal by going on a cruise. His boat was towed by labourers.

IMPACT

The Grand Canal is still in use today. But by 1950 it had silted up so badly that its maximum depth was only 1.8 metres, too shallow for large boats. In the late 1950s, the canal was dredged and widened. Today it is possible for ships weighing up to 2000 tonnes to travel along its length.

FAMOUS PEOPLE

Tradition says that Yu, the Great Engineer who lived about 4000 years ago, was the first person to control China's rivers. He dug channels to irrigate the land and drain away the flood waters. It is said that he was so devoted to his task that he once worked for 13 years without returning home to see his family.

Yu leaving home.

▶ *Harvesting rice in China today. Farming techniques have changed very little in thousands of years.*

A farmer's life

Chinese farmers relied on irrigated farmland to produce enough food to feed their families and pay their taxes to the emperor. Farming was thought so important that farmers, though many were very poor, ranked second in Chinese society, below nobles and scholars. In the north, wheat and millet were the main crops. In the south, rice was grown. For one month a year farmers were forced to work for the emperor, in the army or on building projects.

23

AMAZING MACHINES

Ancient Chinese scientists invented many ingenious devices and machines. Some were practical objects, designed to solve everyday problems and improve people's lives. Others were much more complicated. Many were developed and used in China long before they were known in the rest of the world.

FAMOUS PEOPLE

Zhang Heng was not just a brilliant inventor, but also a skilled mathematician, astronomer, map-maker, painter and poet (see page 16). As Imperial Astronomer he ran the royal observatory where he invented his famous seismograph. In Ancient China, astronomy was an 'official' science. Astronomers were government officials, employed by the emperor.

◄ *The seismograph invented by Zhang Heng in AD 132. It was one of the first instruments made for detecting earthquakes.*

The wheelbarrow was a clever Chinese invention which we still use today. Nicknamed the wooden ox, it was invented in the third century AD. At first, wheelbarrows were used for transporting people and later for carrying goods. They made it possible for people to move heavy loads easily.

An early Chinese wheelbarrow.

▼ *Su Song's astronomical clock invented in about AD 1090.*

Clever collar

A simple, labour-saving Chinese invention was a new type of collar and harness for horses. This collar rested on the horse's chest, rather than on its neck. This meant that horses could pull much heavier loads without choking. It was probably in use by the third century BC. The Ancient Chinese used horses to pull war chariots and farm carts.

Earthquake detective

From ancient times China has suffered terrible earthquakes. The first ever seismograph was invented in AD 132 by Zhang Heng. It was a bronze vase ringed with dragons' heads each with a bronze ball in its mouth. Below each dragon was a toad. Inside the vase was a heavy pendulum which tilted during a tremor so that its top swung towards a dragon, making it drop its ball into the toad's mouth. The centre of the earthquake was worked out to be in the opposite direction. Modern seismographs still work on the pendulum principle.

▲ *An ultra-modern earthquake detection station in the USA. It uses a laser beam to monitor earth movements.*

Water clocks

In about AD 1090, the imperial astronomer Su Song (1020-1101) invented a clock which not only told the time, but also observed the movements of the stars and planets. This information allowed an accurate calendar to be drawn up. The clock was housed inside a tower 10 metres high and powered by a huge waterwheel. Through the day and night, wooden puppets appeared through doors in the clock face. They rang bells and beat drums and gongs to mark the hours. Mechanical clocks were not used in Europe for another 300 years.

EVERYDAY LIFE

Many of the objects invented by the Ancient Chinese for use in their everyday lives spread through trade from China to the rest of the world. Chinese goods were highly sought after. These objects ranged from beautiful porcelain to umbrellas, matches, and the world's first toilet paper! The first matches were made in about the sixth century AD from little sticks of pinewood, coated with sulphur. Toilet paper was made from the sixth century AD onwards for use at the imperial court.

Tea drinking

Today Chinese tea is enjoyed all over the world. It was first drunk in China in about 50 BC when it was used as a medicine to help people stay awake or cure indigestion. During Tang times, tea drinking became very popular and an elaborate ceremony grew up around it. People were encouraged to drink four or five cups of tea a day to cool them down and ease aches and pains.

◄ *A teashop in present-day China. Tea is one of the most popular drinks in the world.*

Keeping off the rain

The first umbrellas were invented in China in about the fourth century AD. They were made from heavy, oiled mulberry paper and protected people from both rain and sun. Blue umbrellas were for ordinary people. The emperor's umbrella was red and yellow. The idea of the umbrella spread from China to India in the fourteenth century. It reached Europe about 400 years later.

Fine china

The Ancient Chinese were skilled craftworkers. The best quality goods were made in the imperial workshops. During the Tang Dynasty, in about AD 900, the Chinese discovered how to make very fine pottery called porcelain. It was hard, shiny and wafer thin, and made a ringing sound when tapped. The famous blue and white porcelain from the Ming Dynasty (1368-1644) is still highly prized today. Porcelain was used to make vases, bowls and figures.

IMPACT

Chopsticks were used in China as early as the third century BC. They were made from wood, bamboo, horn or ivory. Chinese food has changed very little since ancient times when people ate bowls of meat or vegetables, served with rice or millet. Today Chinese food is very popular. Restaurants are found all over the world wherever Chinese people have settled.

A feast in a modern Chinese restaurant.

FAMOUS PEOPLE

Much of our knowledge of everyday life in Ancient China comes from objects found in tombs. One of the most spectacular was the tomb of the wife of the Marquis of Dai, a wealthy Han nobleman. She died in the second century BC and was buried with a huge collection of silk clothes, lacquerware bowls and boxes, musical instruments, pottery figures and even food.

A pottery boat and crew from an early Han tomb.

▼ *An exquisite blue and white Ming porcelain vase.*

FUN AND GAMES

Wealthy people in Ancient China had a great deal of leisure time which they filled with all sorts of entertainments. They loved hunting, polo, soccer and playing cards. Poorer people watched the jugglers, musicians and acrobats who performed in the streets. Many of the toys and games we have today were invented in Ancient China. Playing cards were invented in the ninth century AD. Gambling games were very popular, and large sums of money were bet, won and lost.

A painting of the royal gardens in Beijing.

T'ai Chi

T'ai Chi is a type of martial art which has been practised in China for about 2000 years. Unlike other martial arts, the movements are performed very slowly and gently. The idea is to make your body more flexible and balanced, while also bringing your mind, body and spirit into harmony.

▲ *People doing their morning T'ai Chi exercises. T'ai Chi has become very popular all over the world.*

Flying high

Kites were invented in China in the third century BC. Some were designed as children's toys. Others were fighting kites used in sporting contests. The winner was the owner of the kite which cut through the other's line, bringing it down from the sky. Much stronger kites were used by the army to carry men up to spy on the enemy. Kite-flying is still very popular in China and other parts of Asia, especially at festival times.

▲ *Fireworks light up the night sky in Hong Kong to celebrate the Chinese New Year.*

IMPACT

Soccer, or football, is one of world's most popular sports, both to play and watch. Its ancestor was the Chinese game of t'su chu played in the third century BC. The ball was made of leather and hit with the feet and body, but not the hands. The aim was to strike the ball through a small hole in a silk net.

A fast and furious game of football.

Fabulous fireworks

Gunpowder, invented in AD 1050, was not only used in warfare but also to make fireworks. Different chemicals created different colours when the fireworks exploded. Sparkling trails were made by mixing iron or steel dust with the gunpowder. The most dramatic fireworks were called 'water-rats'. They sped across the water, trailing sparks and flames behind them.

GLOSSARY

alternative Different or unconventional.

anaesthetics Drugs given to a patient to stop them feeling any pain during an operation.

archaeologist A person who studies human history by excavating and examining ruins and remains, such as ancient cities, burial sites and artefacts, such as pots and tools.

assassinate To kill or murder.

astronomy The science of studying the stars, planets and other heavenly bodies.

Buddhism A way of thinking and living begun by an Indian prince, Siddhartha Gautama in the sixth century BC. He spent many years searching for the truth and became the Buddha, or enlightened one. Today there are Buddhists all over the world.

civilization A society which is very advanced in science, technology, the arts, government and law.

cocoon A case spun by a silkworm caterpillar around its body to protect it while it develops into an adult moth.

complementary medicine The same as alternative medicine. A type of medicine which uses natural ingredients from plants or herbs instead of artificial medicines made in a laboratory.

conventional The usual way of doing something.

crossbow A bow with a wooden crossbar in which there is a groove for an arrow.

culture A country or people's achievements in the arts, sciences and technology.

cumbersome Another word for bulky or uncomfortable.

dredge To scoop or clear out mud or silt from the bed of a river or canal.

dynasty A ruling family where power is passed down from one member of the family to another.

economy A country's wealth, including its trade, industry, imports and exports.

emperor The ruler of an empire, a large and powerful state often made up of several countries or territories.

frontier A border between two countries.

grid system A grid of lines running horizontally and vertically across a map, which allows you to pinpoint places and landmarks more accurately.

harmony To be in agreement with something.

hemp A type of plant. Fibres from its stems are spun into yarn and used to make cloth.

ingenious Clever and cunning.

irrigation Supplying fields with a regular water supply so that crops can grow. This might mean digging a channel or ditch to bring water from a nearby river or canal.

jade A hard semi-precious green, white or blue stone, used to make jewellery or ornaments.

kingdom A country or state ruled by a king or queen.

lacquerware A way of decorating wooden objects which was discovered by the Ancient Chinese. Lacquer is liquid made from tree sap. This is heated and mixed with oil, then painted on to bowls and boxes. When laquer dries it becomes very hard and shiny.

magnetic compass An instrument used in navigation which shows you where north is and allows you to find your own position in relation to north.

malaria A tropical disease spread by mosquitoes. Victims suffer from a terrible fever, and can die.

millet A type of cereal plant. Its seeds are ground into flour.

Mongols Nomadic people from the huge plains to the north of China. They conquered northern China in 1279.

mythical To do with myths. A myth is a story which is not based in historical fact but deals with supernatural characters, such as gods and goddesses, their lives and actions.

navigation A way of finding the way from one place to another by plotting a course using instruments such as a compass.

nomads People who do not live settled lives, but move from place to place in search of food and water for themselves and their animals.

observatory A building from which astronomers can observe or watch the skies.

oracle A place, object or person said to be able to tell the future.

parchment A material made out of animal skin. It was used for writing on before paper was invented.

pendulum A weight which hangs and swings freely.

philosopher Someone who studies and thinks about the nature of the universe and the meaning of life.

rotary press A printing press in which the printing plates and paper are wrapped around rollers or cylinders. Rotary describes something which rotates or turns around.

rudder A flat piece of wood or metal fixed to the stern (back) of a ship or boat which is turned from side to side to steer.

saltpeter A white salty substance sometimes used in gunpowder.

seismograph A machine for detecting and recording earthquakes.

silt A muddy mixture of soil, rocks and other materials which collect on the bed of a river or canal, clogging it up or making it more shallow.

stirrups Metal loops used to support a horse rider's feet. This gives the rider a much surer seat.

sulphur A pale yellow chemical with a strong smell which is sometimes used in gunpowder.

surveyor A person who chooses and inspects a site for a building.

terracotta Baked, unglazed, brownish-red clay which is used to make pots and statues.

INDEX